Postcard Views

A Walk Down Main Street
Buffalo, New York, circa 1910

Joseph F. Bieron
Paul J. McCarthy

Edited by
Jennifer Fecio McDougall

BUFFALO
•
HERITAGE
•
UNLIMITED
•

Buffalo, New York

Joseph Bieron, Ph.D., is emeritus professor of chemistry from
Canisius College, Buffalo, New York, and co-founder of
Buffalo Heritage Unlimited.

Paul J. McCarthy, S.J. is a retired Canisius College chemistry
professor who performs his priestly duties at St. Thomas More
parish in Sandy, Utah.

Book Design, Michael Anthony, Buffalo, New York.

Buffalo Heritage Unlimited,
Buffalo, N.Y.
www.buffaloheritage.com
© Copyright 2007

ISBN 978-0-9788476-4-7
Printed in United States of America

To our immigrant grandparents

who, by their hard work, helped shape

the great city of Buffalo.

Entrance to Harbor, Buffalo, N. Y.

12895 CATHOLIC CATHEDRAL, BUFFALO, N. Y.

JOSEPH A. PEPE
GROCERIES

1910

Buffalo Savings Bank, Buffalo, N. Y.

EARLY MORNING
AT CHIPPEWA MARKET, BUFFALO, N. Y.

THE CITY NA

ing North from Shelton Square, Buffalo, N. Y.

IROQUOIS

Contents

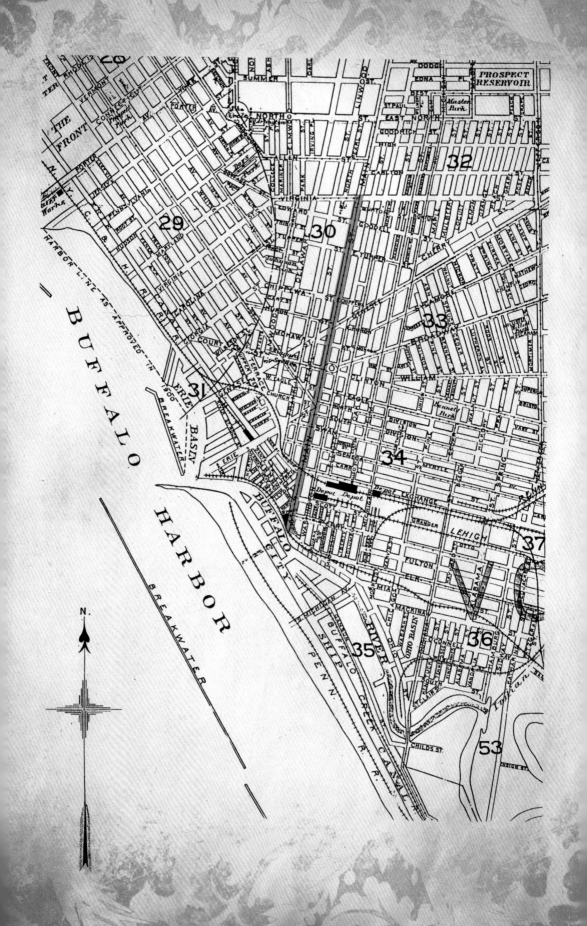

Chapter I

Introduction

In 1900, Buffalo, New York, was the eighth largest city in the United States. As the world ushered in the new century, Buffalo celebrated its status as a vibrant center for transportation, commerce, and industry. Known as the "Gateway to the West," it also became home for thousands of immigrants who chose to begin their new lives in this promising city by the lake.

Postcards erupted on the scene around 1907, a short-lived product of the collision of emerging print technologies and existing postal regulations. This book offers a fascinating and historically accurate glimpse of Buffalo's Main Street in the early 1900s through postcard scenes. Postcards of this era offer a unique slice of Americana, depicting common scenes like streets, parks, office buildings and homes, chronicling the early decades of the past century. These

Elevation of Waterfront, Buffalo, N.Y.
   A panoramic view of Buffalo's waterfront district, at the foot of Main Street. The canal system winds its way between industrial buildings, warehouses and grain mills, and lake freighters appear in the distance. This was the commercial hub of downtown Buffalo.

OFFICIAL SOUVENIR MAILING CARD

ELECTRIC TOWER.

COPYRIGHT, 1901, BY THE NIAGARA ENVELOPE MANUFACTORY   GIES & CO. LITHO. BUFFALO, N.Y. U.S.A.

Official Souvenir Mailing Card Electric Tower
The Electric Tower, soaring to a height of 389 feet, was the
centerpiece of the Pan-American Exposition, held in Buffalo in
1901. Using electricity generated at Niagara Falls, the tower was
illuminated at night by thousands of lights, including dramatic
colored flood lights on a water cascade in front of the tower. Buffalo
became known as "the City of Light."

views of Main Street reveal Buffalo as one of the most progressive and vibrant cities of the time.

Take a walk up Main Street. Start at the Buffalo River and allow Main Street landmarks like the Buffalo Harbor, the Erie Canal, railroads, banks, shops, theaters and churches to tell Buffalo's fabulous story.

The map of downtown Buffalo was reproduced from a 1915 atlas. It shows Main Street in relation to the Buffalo River, Lake Erie, the Erie Canal, and other prominent landmarks. Although details are difficult to discern at this scale, each chapter features a more detailed map of the particular section of Main Street highlighted in that chapter.

History of the Postcard

In 1913, approximately 968 million postcards were sent by mail in the United States. However, the nation's population was less than 100 million at that time. This means that every man, woman and child sent an average of ten postcards each! And Americans were not alone in their affection for the humble postcard – residents of Germany sent a total of nearly 1.2 billion postcards in 1906! The picture postcard craze was at its peak during these heady years.

Although a simple postcard for sending a message or an advertisement was copyrighted in the U.S. in 1861, the postcard did not catch on immediately. An 1865 effort to make postcards commonplace elsewhere in the world also failed when the Austro-German Postal Conference declined to act on a proposal for an "open post-sheet" (offenes Postblatt). The concept, however, resurfaced in Austria in 1869. Emmanuel Hermann was responsible for resurrecting the idea and his timing was clearly right. When the Austrian government issued these correspondence cards, three million sold in just the first three months!

Many countries around the world introduced postcards between 1871 and 1873. The U.S. joined the ranks in 1873 with a simple, unadorned card: one side was blank and the other side contained a printed one-cent stamp and a place to write the recipient's address. It was a government monopoly of sorts: although private cards could be used, they required two cents postage. Most of these early postcards were used for advertising.

The origins of the picture postcard are a bit murkier. One of the first known pictorial postcards was postmarked in Basle, Switzerland, in 1865. Later examples include postcards postmarked in England during the 1870 Christmas season and "viewcards" found in Germany in the 1870s. Many of the early German postcards offered Gruss aus... or "Greetings from" the location depicted on the postcard.

Souvenir picture postcards appeared in the U.S. in time for the Columbian Exposition in Chicago in 1893. On these early cards, the message from the sender had to be written on the same side as the picture. By law, the other side of the card was reserved for the address of the recipient. No space was provided for a return address.

Prior to 1898, there were three kinds of postcards: advertising postcards, exposition issues and viewcards. These are now known as pioneer postcards. Then, a change in the postal regulations governing postcards on May 19, 1898, changed everything. It allowed privately

Official Souvenir Mailing Card Albright Art Gallery
The Albright Art Gallery was one of just two permanent buildings designed for the Pan-American Exposition. Although it was designed by Green & Wicks to stand at the entrance of the Exposition grounds, it was not completed in time and instead opened after the Exposition closed. The building still stands and is listed in the National Register of Historic Places.

Official Souvenir Mailing Card Ethnology Building
The Ethnology Building was designed by noted architect George Cary. It was located across an esplanade from the Temple of Music, and the two buildings were similar in design. The Ethnology Building exhibits featured archeological artifacts from throughout the Americas.

Main Street Looking North, Buffalo, N.Y.
Postcards with views of Shelton Square were very popular among Buffalo fans of early picture postcards. Dated August 15, 1905, but postmarked October 16, 1905, this postcard offers proof of the vitality and life on this important section of Main Street during the early 1900s.

published postcards to be mailed under the same conditions as official postcards. The postage for any type of postcard was just one cent. Privately published cards bore the following inscription: "Private Mailing Card authorized by Act of Congress of May 19, 1898."

Souvenir postcards were printed for the Pan-American Exposition held in Buffalo in 1901. Labeled "Official Souvenir Mailing Card," they are classified as Private Mailing Cards (PMCs) by postcard collectors. The postcards were copyrighted by the Niagara Envelope Manufactory of Buffalo. The back of the cards bore the notation "Private Mailing Card authorized by Congress May 19, 1898," and was marked "Postal Card – Carte Postale." The back of the cards was reserved by law for the recipient's address and the postage was one cent. Three fine examples of these souvenir cards feature Exposition scenes.

Main Street, Buffalo, N. Y.

Main Street, Buffalo, N.Y.
This view northward showcases the 400 block of Main Street. The bustling shopping district scene includes AM&A's in the foreground, and the H.A. Meldrum Co. department store and Victor Furniture in the background.

The use of the term "postcard" was not granted to private printers by the U.S. government until December 4, 1901. Writing was still not permitted on the side reserved for the recipient's address, but space was usually left on the picture side to write a short message. Postcards featuring images of Main Street scenes with writing on the front are examples of postcards postmarked between 1901 and 1907.

A new era in postcards in the United States began in 1907. A change in postal regulations allowed the back of the cards to be divided. This made it possible to include a message on the left side, reserving the right side for the recipient's address and the stamp. The reverse side could then be completely devoted to the picture.

The "divided back era" in postcards encompasses 1907 through 1914. Most of the postcards displayed in this book were printed during this postcard heyday.

The first "Entrance to Harbor" postcard was printed prior to this era, while the second postcard of the same scene was printed during the divided back era; the difference between pre-1907 and post-1907 postcards is quite apparent.

Main Street, Buffalo, N.Y.
Browning King and Co., a clothing store at 575 Main Street between Genesee and Chippewa streets, dominates this view of the Shopping District. Postmarked April 6, 1906.

Lithography was an important part of the art of making high-quality color postcards, but the entire process was a well-kept secret in the early days. In lithography, limestone was ground to a level surface and treated with soaplike substances called fatty acids. The fatty acids bound to the stone and made its surface water repellent but organic-dye absorbent. The surface was engraved with an image and the dyes were absorbed onto the stone's surface. The single dye image was transferred to the paper card stock. Each color required a separate stone and twenty stones were commonly used. German lithographic printers, who set the mark for high standards, used as many as forty different stones, or colors.

The postcard craze, which hit the U.S. during the first two decades of the century, peaked between 1902 and 1913. In fact, during this period, postcard albums were found in most parlors, much as photo albums have long been a staple of American coffee tables. Used judiciously, postcard albums entertained guests; they could also be quite tedious when presented too relentlessly by the host.

Until 1914, the best picture postcards were printed in Germany, but the Great War (World War I) put an end to this practice. The influenza epidemic of 1918, combined with supply shortages caused by the war, drove the postcard craze into a steep decline. Add to this the development of the relatively inexpensive Kodak camera, which made it possible for people

Entrance to the Harbor, Buffalo, N.Y.

Entrance to the Harbor, Buffalo, N.Y.
This view of the entrance to Buffalo Harbor shows the DL&W Railroad coal trestle on the left and the grain elevators along the Buffalo River in the background. Postmarked August 12, 1906.

Entrance to Harbor, Buffalo, N. Y.

Entrance to the Harbor, Buffalo, N.Y.
Postmarked February, 1911, this view of the entrance to Buffalo Harbor also shows the DL&W Railroad coal trestle on the left and the grain elevators along the Buffalo River in the background. However, between the 1906 Harbor entrance postcard and this one, postal regulation changes provided space on the back of the card for a message and the overall quality of postcards improved significantly.

to take their own pictures of scenes worth recording, and the end of the craze was in the cards. Although color film was still a long way off, the personal nature of these Kodak photographs was captivating to many people. The result was that interest in postcards further declined. Even though they were in color, the images had been captured by others.

Postcards printed in the U.S. between 1915 and 1930 were not nearly as nice as the earlier ones colorized in Germany. Most had a white border surrounding the picture, like the two showing "Main St. looking North." But the quality soared between 1930 and 1945 once paper with a higher rag content began to be used. This allowed bright dyes to be used to color the black and white pictures, and postcards suddenly became quite popular again. A further improvement in postcard quality arrived with the introduction of the "photochrome" in 1939. This process produced great photos for a fraction of the cost. Although postcard production and use slumped somewhat during World War II, photochrome postcards came to dominate the scene after 1945 and provided a new impetus for the use of picture postcards.

Early Buffalo

The Johnson family arrived in 1784 as the first white settlers in the area now known as Buffalo. Real settlement began, however, with the purchase of a large swath of the western part of New York State by the Holland Land Company in 1790. Surveyor Joseph Ellicott drew up plans for New Amsterdam, a town to be located on Buffalo Creek.

In 1804, there were approximately twenty houses in the town, now named Buffalo. By 1812, the town had grown to a population of approximately fifteen hundred people. On December 30, 1813, however, a band of British soldiers and their Indian allies crossed the Niagara River from Fort Erie, landed on Squaw Island and made their way to Buffalo. A battle ensued and several houses were set on fire. The conflagration quickly spread, and when it was finally extinguished, only seven houses still stood. Buffalo's determined settlers rebuilt their town, and by 1820, the population had risen to more than two thousand hearty souls.

The opening of the Erie Canal on October 26, 1825, contributed mightily to the growth of Buffalo over the next decade. This shallow feat of engineering stretching more than 360 miles provided an inexpensive way to ship raw materials from the west to the manufacturing centers of the east. And it was just as inexpensive to ship the finished products back to the west where the demand for them was rapidly growing. Buffalo was the hub of all of this burgeoning shipping activity, a fact which led to rapid growth and development.

Buffalo Light House, Buffalo, N. Y.

Buffalo Light House, Buffalo, N.Y.
The Buffalo Light House stands at the entrance to the Buffalo River. It was built in 1833 and has stood sentinel over the rise and fall of Buffalo's waterfront and downtown for nearly 175 years. It is one of the oldest structures still standing in the city.

"Italians. There are a large number of them in Buffalo, largely laborers, rag-pickers and fruit venders. They are industrious but dirty as a rule, and while they often present a miserable appearance and suffer privations it is not usually because they are so poor, but rather that they prefer to hoard their money. There are perhaps, some organ grinders among them and indeed musicians of a higher order. They are apt to form settlements by themselves and are to be found in the tenements at the foot of Main Street, on Genesee near the canal; and in and about the Terrace. They are commonly sober but when intoxicated are extremely quarrelsome and their localities are often the scene of a stabbing affray. As a rule the children of these people are turned out to earn a penny at an early age, and these little street waifs sell papers, black boots or beg, seeming to fear nothing and preferring a street life to any other."

The paternal grandfather of the authors (JFB) was born in Poland and his maternal grandparents were born in Italy. Speaking from personal knowledge, prejudice does not diminish strong will and character.

Main Street looking North, Buffalo, N.Y.
This excellent photograph of Main Street looking north from Shelton Square clearly shows what Kleinhans, J. N. Adam & Co., the Palace Theatre and the Bank of Buffalo once looked like.

Main Street looking North, Buffalo, N.Y.
Another, later view of Main Street looking north from Shelton Square showcases the Liberty Building, built in 1925 with a replica Statue of Liberty on each peaked roof. The large red building on the right, once the Iroquois Hotel, has by this time already become the Bramson Building.

When the canal opened, the population of Buffalo numbered approximately twenty-four hundred, but when the town was incorporated just seven years later in 1832, the population had grown to more than ten thousand. At that time, Buffalo boasted forty manufacturing companies and sixteen schools. The Erie Canal was a driving force in the growth of commerce on the Great Lakes, leading to significant improvements to the Buffalo harbor.

Then came the railroads. The number of rail lines that entered Buffalo or passed through it skyrocketed in the 1830s and continued to multiply through the last half of the nineteenth century. Buffalo became a transportation hub for both passenger and freight service. Literally millions of cattle, sheep and horses moved through the city en route to slaughterhouses and tanneries. The consolidation of smaller lines into giants like the New York Central allowed for the extensive improvement of track and terminal facilities, helping railroads take over most of the traffic that once flowed on the canal. The railroad became king in Buffalo in the early years of the twentieth century.

Buffalo was once one of the fastest-growing cities in the United States, initially in area, and then in population and commercial importance. In 1832, Buffalo covered just four and a half square miles; by 1854, it had expanded tenfold to forty-two square miles.

Until the latter part of the nineteenth century, Buffalo was largely a city of commerce. The introduction of natural gas as a fuel source in 1884 was the first major step toward industrialization. The advent of electric power from Niagara Falls in 1896 was the next step, and actually eclipsed the importance of natural gas. The Pan-American Exposition in 1901, attended by eight million people, showcased to the world Buffalo's significance as a center of industrial power.

When the Lackawanna Steel plant opened in 1903, it immediately became the largest and most complete steel plant in the world. In 1900, Buffalo boasted the eighth largest population of all U.S. cities. By 1925, it was recognized as eighth in the nation as measured by the value of products manufactured locally.

The vast waves of immigrants from Europe fueled this tremendous growth. Buffalo was originally settled by the English, who filtered down from New England, then by early German immigrants, followed by the Irish who worked on the waterfront. In the 1880s, Italian immigrants populated the city's west side and the Canal district on the waterfront, while Eastern Europeans, primarily from Poland, settled on the city's east side. By 1900, Buffalo was a city of distinct ethnic neighborhoods, as were so many large cities in the northeast at the time.

This is the vibrant, colorful city that Main Street graced in Buffalo during the early 1900s. There was great wealth, unlimited business opportunities, a rapidly growing population, a unique geographic location and unprecedented technological development. Postcards from the era tell this tale in a unique and fascinating fashion.

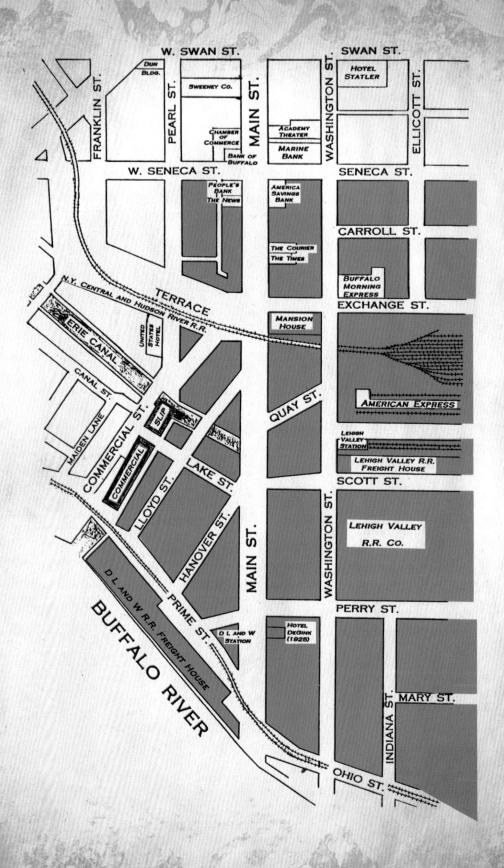

Chapter 2

Lower Main Street:
the Transportation Hub

The Buffalo Harbor was a major transportation hub in Buffalo. Grain elevators lined the banks of the Buffalo River, which saw heavy water traffic, including tug boats and lake freighters. At the turn of the twentieth century, one could stand at the foot of Main Street and see the Erie Canal, lake steamers and freighters, railroads and electric streetcars, and horse-drawn carriages.

The foot of Main Street was unique in Buffalo as the point at which all forms of transportation converged: the Erie Canal met up with lake steamers and freighters, railroads, and the city transport of horse cars or streetcars. The crowd pictured on the postcard at the foot of Main Street on the Buffalo River (on page 16) is waiting to board the Americana, an excursion boat to Crystal Beach. The postmark on the back of this card indicates that the picture was taken prior to 1912.

Buffalo Harbor, Buffalo, N.Y.
The Buffalo River, looking east from the Michigan Avenue Bridge. The GLF grain elevator, in the foreground to the right, was demolished in 1909.

The Foot of Main Street, Buffalo, N.Y. postcard on page 18, is full of interesting information about the era. Note the billboard advertising the Enquirer, a local daily newspaper. Another sign offers a surprise: an advertisement for Tobler's Swiss chocolate. This company remains today one of the most renowned makers of fine chocolates in Switzerland. The D. L. & W. passenger terminal and freight house, located at 40 Main Street, can be seen off to the left. The rails crossed Main at street level at the time of the postcard, but the tracks are not visible in this view. The rear of the D. L. & W. terminal abutted the railroad tracks.

The vibrancy of this downtown hub is apparent. Main Street from its starting point all the way to Scajaquada Creek (Delavan) had been electrified since 1891 and streetcars are visible in the distance. In fact, within a short time, this Main Street service was extended to the city line. Although the postcard on page 18 is postmarked 1910, the picture is obviously an earlier

Boat Landing at the Foot of Main Street, Buffalo, N.Y.
The Americana, which, along with the Canadiana, carried thousands of passengers to the Crystal Beach amusement park in Canada. When not transporting passengers, the boats were docked at the foot of Main Street.

view since all of the small vehicles are horse-drawn. This view of Main Street also features an office where it appears that travel to Detroit can be arranged, and there is a store marked First Chance. Cigars were popular in those days and the billboard in the upper right offers products for those who smoked them, as well as advertising wines and liquors. It is not known what the Enterprise legend on the building on the right side of the picture refers to.

The Mansion House (postcard on page 19) was a prominent Buffalo hotel for those who worked in transportation at that time. Located at 169 Main Street, mere blocks from the transportation hub at the foot of Main Street, the hotel was accessible to people arriving by boat or train. The Mansion House had 244 rooms and the rates in 1896 started at $2.50 a day!

Some historians have speculated that the hotel may have been named the Mansion House because the first frame house ever constructed on the site was known as the Mansion. The original dwelling was built in the first decade of the nineteenth century by Samuel Pratt. It stood on the north side of Exchange Street (then called Crow) at Main. After several name changes, the hotel property was finally named the Mansion House in 1825. The hotel was rebuilt in 1843 and additional renovations were completed in 1846. Other significant changes followed, including an expansion to six stories in 1883.

Although the Mansion House was a brick building, it was not fireproof. Many similar hotels, in fact, were destroyed by fire. The American Hotel, for example, which had opened in 1836 between Eagle and Court streets, was actually destroyed twice by fire. The first fire occurred in 1850 and the second in 1865. The Mansion House was demolished in November 1932. A parking lot occupies the site today.

Many railroads passed through downtown Buffalo and branched out in every direction, as seen on pages 20 and 21. The New York Central Railroad was the most prominent; its terminal was on Exchange Street. The Lehigh Valley Railroad terminal was built in 1916-1917 on Main Street, on the site now occupied by the Donovan Building, with its rail yards stretching eastward.

The D. L. & W. freight house was on the Buffalo River just east of Main Street. The Lehigh Valley R.R. freight house was on Scott Street running east from Washington Street. The freight house of the NYC and Hudson River R.R. was located just north of that.

The train shed of the D. L. & W. passenger terminal, built in 1917, stands in Buffalo today as a landmark and a nod to the city's rail history. Currently, this building is used as a terminus and maintenance barn for the subway line of Buffalo's Niagara Frontier Transportation Authority (NFTA).

Buffalo had an extensive trolley system known as the Buffalo Railway Co., which dated to 1860 when ground was broken for the first tracks. Early lines were limited to Main and Niagara streets but additional lines were added over time. Gas lighting in the trolley cars initially offered dim light, and cars were unheated. The introduction of electricity in 1891 greatly improved conditions for trolley riders and the horse-drawn cars were soon replaced by electric trolley cars.

CRYSTAL BEACH

Crystal Beach is on the Canadian shore of Lake Erie, about ten miles from Buffalo.

For many years, it was a family resort – as of 1896, liquor was not even permitted. In addition to swimming, boating and fishing facilities, there were also restaurants and lunch counters, a picnic grove, a bowling alley, a shooting gallery, a merry-go-round, a toboggan slide, a dance pavilion and even a barber shop! A large hotel had a dining room open to both day visitors and longterm residents. Later, other amusements and rides were added to the vast array of activities already available, including the historic Comet roller coaster.

A ferry trip and a train ride made Crystal Beach accessible to Buffalonians, but most folks sailed over in style on one of the excursion boats. In 1896, a fleet of boats named Garden City, Pearl and Gazelle made as many as twelve round trips a day during the summer. In 1912, the Americana and the Canadiana were the most popular boats for the forty-five-minute trip. A riot on board the Canadiana in 1956 put a quick end to this genteel era.

The 101-year-old amusement park at Crystal Beach closed on Labor Day, 1989.

Buffalo's trolley service was gradually upgraded: new lines were added to meet demand and equipment was replaced and upgraded when possible. The service even grew to serve communities beyond the city's limits, including Kenmore, Niagara Falls and Lockport. A merger in 1902 united all of the existing lines under the auspices of the International Railway Co.

Foot of Main Street, Buffalo, N.Y.
The foot of Main Street, with the D. L. & W. tracks on the left and trolleys traveling up Main, was a transportation center in the early 1900s. Postmarked August 4, 1910.

The transportation of grain and flour as it passed from the Midwestern states to consumers in the east was a major industry in Buffalo. The massive grain elevators that line the Buffalo River were where untold tons of grain were unloaded and stored and later transferred to railroad cars.

The Erie Canal was seventy-five years old in 1900, and it had been greatly improved in width and depth. Still, it had lost most of its business to the railroads by this time. However, for heavy materials that did not need to reach a destination quickly, such as construction materials, the canal system still provided a useful alternative.

Mansion House, Buffalo, N.Y.
The Mansion House, a 244-room hotel for traveling men. This six-story inn at Exchange and Washington streets was convenient to the city's train depots.

Grain Elevators, Buffalo, N.Y.
The Buffalo River lined with grain elevators as lake-going vessels unload their cargo from the Midwest. Buffalo was the nation's second-largest grain center at the turn of the last century.

85 D. L. & W. Terminal, Buffalo, N. Y.

D. L. & W. Terminal, Buffalo, N.Y.
The classically elegant new D. L. & W. terminal replaced the modest terminal shown on page 18 (Foot of Main Street, Buffalo, N.Y.). Freight was handled at river level and passengers were served at street level.

New York Central Depot, Buffalo, N.Y.

New York Central Depot, Buffalo, N.Y.
The first New York Central Depot, on Exchange Street two blocks east of Main, was one of several passenger train depots close to Main Street

Train Shed, N. Y. Central, Buffalo, N. Y.

Train Shed, N. Y. Central, Buffalo, N.Y.
The New York Central railroad passenger service yards, east of the New York Central Depot on Exchange Street. This view looks west toward Main Street. The depot tower is to the right of center and the Michigan Avenue bridge can be seen in the background.

Scene along the Erie Canal at Buffalo, N.Y.
The Erie Canal, which entered downtown Buffalo and ended at Main Street where it connected with the Buffalo River. Barges were towed by teams of mules. The Holloway Point Abino Sand Company and the Erie County Penitentiary can be seen in the background.

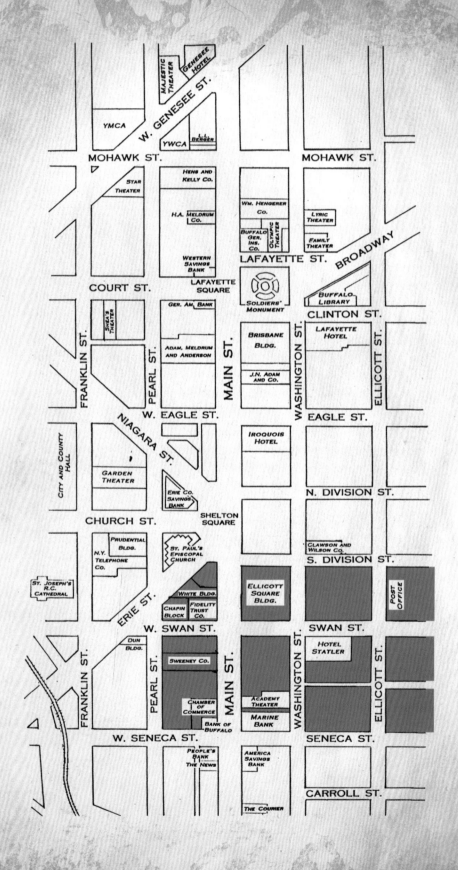

Chapter 3

The Business District:
Seneca Street to Shelton Square

Today, the block of Main Street between Exchange and Seneca streets is occupied by the massive HSBC Building, which straddles Main Street. At the turn of the last century, however, several newspapers were published on this block.

North on Main Street from Seneca Street, Buffalo, N.Y.

The intersection of Seneca and Main streets, the nexus of Buffalo's banking district. A bit of research reveals that this postcard image must have been captured between 1905 and 1913. The People's Bank moved to the southeast corner in 1905; however, a 1915 map shows that it later moved to the southwest corner. The new Marine Bank on the northeast corner was built in 1912-1913. The Bank of Buffalo is on the northwest corner and the Ellicott Square Building is in the background.

In 1915, the Times was published at 193 Main Street, the Courier at 197 Main Street, and the News just across the way at 218 Main Street. The Buffalo Morning Express was also nearby, on the northeast corner of Washington and Exchange streets. Proximity to the nearby railway freight yards accounts for this concentration of publishing ventures, as it allowed the tons of paper needed to be delivered daily. This block was also strategically situated between the busy transportation section of Main Street and the business district, where many prominent citizens spent their days.

Banks dominated the bustling business district, clustered along the Seneca Street, Swan Street and Ellicott Square blocks of Main. The 1915 Atlas of Buffalo reveals that all four corners of Main and Seneca were occupied by banks: the American Savings Bank on the southeast corner, the People's Bank on the southwest corner, Marine Bank on the northeast corner, and the Bank of Buffalo on the northwest corner. Amazingly enough, the same was true just one block north, at the corner of Main and Swan: Third National Bank was located on the southeast corner, Manufacturers and Traders' Trust on the southwest corner, the Ellicott Square Building on the northeast corner, and Fidelity Trust Co. on the northwest corner.

Chamber of Commerce Bldg., Buffalo, N. Y.

More banks were located further north along Main Street: the Erie County Savings Bank was at Shelton Square, the German American Bank (later renamed Liberty Bank) and Western Savings Bank were both on Court Street, and the Buffalo Savings Bank was on Genesee Street.

Many of the most prominent citizens of Buffalo were officers at these banks, a few of which still stand today.

Chamber of Commerce Bldg., Buffalo, N.Y.
The Bank of Buffalo building is dwarfed by the ten-story Chamber of Commerce Building. The Bank of Buffalo, established in 1873, built this building in 1895 on the original site of the bank. It later moved to the northeast corner of Main and North Division streets.

Main Street, Looking North from Seneca Street, Buffalo, N.Y.

Main and Seneca streets from a different vantage point, illustrating Buffalo's banking center before the fourteen-story Marine Bank was built in 1913. The domed Bank of Buffalo is adjacent to the much taller Chamber of Commerce building, and the tall building on the west side opposite the gray Ellicott Square Building is the Fidelity Trust Co. Postmarked July 16, 1912.

Federal Building, Buffalo, N.Y.

The architecturally magnificent Federal Post Office Building, constructed between 1894 and 1901, is two blocks east of Main Street, bounded by Swan, Ellicott, South Division and Oak streets.

Main Street, Buffalo, N.Y.
Swan Street, one block north of Seneca Street. The Third National Bank building can be seen at 273 Main Street, and the Ellicott Square Building occupies the entire city block bounded by Main, South Division, Washington and Swan streets. At the time of its construction in 1895, the Ellicott Square Building was the largest office building in the world.

Main Street from Chamber of Commerce, Buffalo, N.Y.
Main Street, beyond the Ellicott Square Building to the Iroquois Hotel at Main and Eagle streets. In between is Shelton Square, one of the hubs of Joseph Ellicott's design for the city.

The Ellicott Square Building is one of the premier architectural gems in Buffalo, a city of architectural renown. It was built precisely where Joseph Ellicott had planned to build his own residence when he surveyed and designed the city for the Holland Land Company. It is ten stories high, and features a spectacular atrium in the center. When it was built in 1895-1896, it was the largest office building in the world. It anchored the corner of Shelton Square, one of the most prominent city crossroads in 1910, and still dominates this section of Main Street.

Marine 'Nat'l. Bank Bldg., Buffalo, N. Y.

Marine National Bank Building, Buffalo, N.Y.
The fourteen-story Marine National Bank, built in 1913. Organized in 1850 and originally located on lower Main Street, the bank moved to 220 Main Street and then built this significant structure across the street. It remains a prominent office building today at Main and Seneca streets.

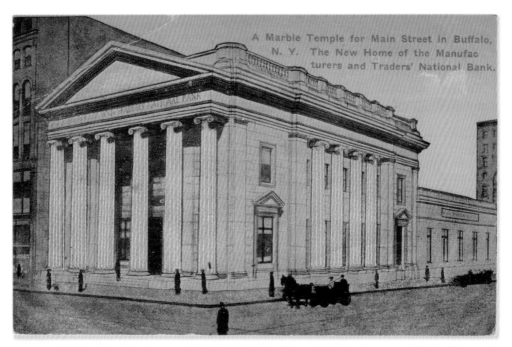

A Marble Temple for Main Street in Buffalo, N.Y. The New Home of the Manufacturers and Traders' National Bank

The Manufacturers and Traders' National Bank, one of the earliest banks in Buffalo, was at the corner of Main, Swan and Pearl streets, just one block south of Shelton Square.

City Hall, Buffalo, N.Y.

City and County Hall was built between 1871 and 1876, two blocks west of Main Street. The building is bounded by Church, Franklin and West Eagle streets and Delaware Avenue and still serves Erie County government today.

Catholic Cathedral, Buffalo, N.Y.

St. Joseph's Cathedral was constructed in 1851 through 1855 by Bishop John Timon, the first Catholic bishop of Buffalo. It is located on Franklin Street, two blocks west of Main Street in the heart of the business district.

Delaware Ave., showing McKinley Monument in distance, Buffalo, N.Y.

Close to the main business district was Delaware Avenue, the grand avenue of Buffalo, where many wealthy, prominent citizens maintained magnificent homes. It was a beautiful, tree-lined residential road before heavy automobile traffic necessitated uprooting the trees to widen the street.

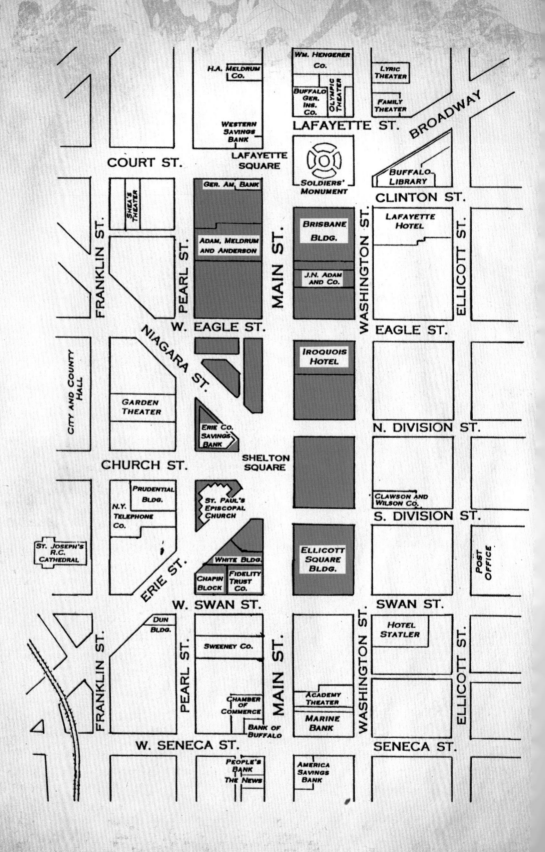

COURT ST.

H.A. MELDRUM CO.

WESTERN SAVINGS BANK

LAFAYETTE SQUARE

LAFAYETTE ST.

WM. HENGERER CO.

BUFFALO GER. INS. CO.

OLYMPIC THEATER

LYRIC THEATER

FAMILY THEATER

BROADWAY

SOLDIERS' MONUMENT

BUFFALO LIBRARY

CLINTON ST.

FRANKLIN ST.

SHEA'S THEATER

GER. AM. BANK

ADAM, MELDRUM AND ANDERSON

PEARL ST.

MAIN ST.

WASHINGTON ST.

BRISBANE BLDG.

J.N. ADAM AND CO.

LAFAYETTE HOTEL

ELLICOTT ST.

EAGLE ST.

W. EAGLE ST.

NIAGARA ST.

CITY AND COUNTY HALL

GARDEN THEATER

ERIE CO. SAVINGS BANK

IROQUOIS HOTEL

N. DIVISION ST.

CHURCH ST.

SHELTON SQUARE

S. DIVISION ST.

CLAWSON AND WILSON CO.

PRUDENTIAL BLDG.

N.Y. TELEPHONE CO.

ST. PAUL'S EPISCOPAL CHURCH

ST. JOSEPH'S R.C. CATHEDRAL

ERIE ST.

WHITE BLDG.

CHAPIN BLOCK

FIDELITY TRUST CO.

ELLICOTT SQUARE BLDG.

POST OFFICE

W. SWAN ST.

SWAN ST.

DUN BLDG.

SWEENEY CO.

HOTEL STATLER

CHAMBER OF COMMERCE

BANK OF BUFFALO

ACADEMY THEATER

MARINE BANK

SENECA ST.

W. SENECA ST.

PEOPLE'S BANK THE NEWS

AMERICA SAVINGS BANK

Chapter 4

SHELTON SQUARE

Shelton Square was a significant point of convergence in Joseph Ellicott's design of the city. Three important avenues from the west: Niagara Street, Church Street and Erie Street, met Main Street to form an important business hub. Very early in the city's history, churches dominated the square and were a vital part of the social fabric of Buffalo. Hotels were then built to accommodate the large volume of travelers passing through the city on their way westward and the many visitors who came to conduct business and experience Buffalo's vitality and exuberance.

During the first decade of the 1900s, Buffalo was a prime destination for conventions of national organizations, which brought many visitors to the city. In 1901, the Pan-American Exposition alone attracted eight million visitors.

Shelton Square, Buffalo, N.Y.
St. Paul's Cathedral and the Prudential (Guaranty) Building shown here are both National Historic Landmarks today. Note the presence of electric street cars. These represented advanced technology in 1909, the year this postcard was postmarked.

The new Statler Hotel

The grandeur of the original Statler Hotel at Washington and Swan Streets was surpassed only by that of the new Statler Hotel on Delaware Avenue at Niagara Square.

Ground was broken for the new construction on May 18, 1921, at the site of what was originally the circa 1850 home of James Hollister. President Millard Fillmore subsequently purchased the property and resided there until his death in 1874, after which his son sold it, and the new owner made extensive renovations to allow the property to be used as a hotel.

Initially known as the Hotel Fillmore and subsequently renamed the Castle Inn, the hotel was able to accommodate 250 guests. Construction of the new Statler Hotel on this site lasted two years and the new hotel opened on May 18, 1923.

Like the original hotel, the new Statler drew international acclaim. It cost more than $8 million to build and rose 265 feet over the city. Its 1,170 rooms could accommodate 2,500 guests, and it featured extraordinary amenities including private bathrooms for every room.

As the postcard street scenes clearly illustrate, merchants lined Main Street with stores, businesses of every nature filled the Ellicott Square Building, and numerous banks completed the thriving commercial district.

Because Shelton Square no longer exists, it is difficult to understand its prominence during the postcard era. Many of the stores, along with the Erie County Savings Bank and the street intersections, have been replaced by Main Place Mall on the west side and M&T Plaza on the east side of Main Street, and the above-ground rapid transit system has eliminated street traffic on Main Street. With

Hotel Statler, Buffalo, N.Y.
Buffalo's original Hotel Statler, on the southeast corner of Washington and Swan streets, one block from Main Street. The building became the Hotel Buffalo. The ballpark that is home to the AAA baseball team, the Buffalo Bisons, stands on this site today.

the decline of many downtown businesses, the area bears little or no resemblance to Shelton Square at the turn of the last century.

Churches were the earliest and most prominent buildings at this busy crossroads. The First Presbyterian Church, constructed in 1823, was situated on a triangular parcel in a block bordered by Main, Church, Pearl and Niagara streets. The frame structure of the original church was replaced in 1827 with a red brick building which stood on the site until 1891 and was known as the "Old First Church." The property was sold to the Erie County Savings Bank when the church's operations moved to a site at Wadsworth and Pennsylvania avenues. A new church, designed by Green & Wicks, was built at that location and inaugural services were held on December 31, 1891.

The congregation of St. Paul's Episcopal Church came together for the first time in February 1817. The initial meeting took place in Elias Ransom's tavern at the corner of Main and Huron. A sizable number of Buffalonians counted themselves among the earliest congregants of St. Paul's Episcopal Church. Of the approximately one hundred homes in Buffalo at the time, residents of around twenty were members of the church.

The congregation soon moved from Ransom's tavern to the Eagle Tavern, on the west side of Main south of Court Street. Later, services were held in the schoolhouse on Niagara Street near Main. St. Paul's Episcopal Church eventually acquired a more permanent home when a church was built on a triangular lot bordered by Main, Church and Erie streets donated by the Holland Land Company.

St. Paul's initially had several pastors in quick succession. That changed with the arrival of thirty-one-year-old Reverend William Shelton. Reverend Shelton preached his first sermon as pastor of St. Paul's on September 13, 1829, and served as pastor until January 1881.

A new church was constructed during Reverend Shelton's tenure. Although the church was built in 1849 and consecrated on October 22, 1851, it took an additional twenty-two years to finish adding the spires and pinnacles for which St. Paul's Episcopal Church is now known. Richard Upjohn, architect of New York City's Trinity Church, designed St. Paul's. Upjohn's design is early English Gothic in brown stone. A complete restoration was done immediately following a major fire in the church in May 1888.

Reverend Shelton died in Connecticut on October 11, 1883. Several years later, around 1890, the section of Buffalo often known as "The Churches" area was renamed Shelton Square in his honor.

Although St. Joseph's Catholic Church, commonly known as St. Joseph's Cathedral, is not located on Main Street, it was part of the Churches district. The cornerstone of this Buffalo landmark was laid on February 6, 1851, by Bishop John Timon. The church was dedicated on July 1, 1855.

Hotels were also very prominent around and near Shelton Square. As a thriving city with a growing population and a bustling commercial center, Buffalo hosted visitors from across the country and around the world. This translated into a significant demand for hotel rooms. Just as in modern times, hotels ranged from simple rooms to luxurious accommodations with every available amenity. Buffalo's Statler Hotel most definitely fell into the latter category.

Main Street, Looking North from Shelton Square, Buffalo, N.Y.
The east side of Main Street, including Shelton Square, in 1901. This was a very popular postcard for many years. This area is known today as One M&T Plaza.

Built by Ellsworth M. Statler, the stately thirteen-story original Statler Hotel opened on January 18, 1908. The hotel occupied the parcel of land at the corner of Washington and Swan streets where St. John's Episcopal Church once stood. Construction of the church had been completed in 1848; it was sold in 1903 and razed in 1906 to make way for the hotel. Shortly thereafter, Statler purchased and razed the Hotel Richelieu, located immediately to the east of the church parcel, and used the additional land to enlarge his hotel.

Buffalo, N.Y., Shelton Square

The west side of Shelton Square in 1906. This was one of the most popular postcard views of the day. St. Paul's Cathedral is pictured here, along with the Prudential (Guaranty) Building and the Erie County Savings Bank, no longer standing.

Main and Niagara Streets, Buffalo, N.Y.

The northwest side of Shelton Square, with Niagara Street in the left corner. Although the card is postmarked April 22, 1912, the picture was taken at an earlier time.

The Statler opened with 450 rooms, making it the largest hotel in Buffalo. It was something of an international wonder, as well, as it featured a bath in every room! Hoteliers came from all over the world to visit the Statler, which had a profound influence on future hotel design and construction. Among its many notable guests, the Statler hosted three U.S. presidents: Theodore Roosevelt, William Howard Taft and Woodrow Wilson.

The Iroquois Hotel at 369 Main Street was an eight-story brown stone and brick construction built by the Buffalo Library Association at a cost of $1 million. The most notable feature of the Iroquois, which opened on August 13, 1889, was that it was completely fireproofed. Given the devastating history of structure fires in Buffalo and other cities, this distinction was very important for Buffalonians. The American Hotel, on Main Street between Eagle and Court had been destroyed not once, but twice by fire, first in 1850 and then again in 1865.

Iroquois Hotel
Buffalo, N. Y.

The Iroquois, which extended from Main to Washington along Eagle Street, could accommodate as many as five hundred guests. Three stories were added in 1901 to prepare for the Pan-American Exposition, increasing the hotel's size by 150 rooms and 45 baths. By 1908, the hotel was able to accommodate six hundred guests and the expansive dining rooms provided seating for five hundred people!

The Hotel Statler Company assumed ownership of the Iroquois Hotel on June 30, 1922, and promptly announced that it planned to convert it into an office building. The Iroquois ceased to function as a hotel on May 17, 1923, the day before the new Statler Hotel opened its doors. Statler

Iroquois Hotel, Buffalo, N.Y.
The Iroquois Hotel, on the southeast corner of Main and Eagle streets.
The hotel opened in 1889 and extensive renovations were done in 1901 in
anticipation of the Pan-American Exposition. It closed on May 17, 1923.

Modern Woodmen Foresters Parade, Buffalo, N.Y., June 1911

Hundreds of Buffalonians watching a parade on Main Street in 1911 – probably one of many, as parades were very popular in Buffalo during this period. The Rienzi Hotel can be seen on the west side of Main Street.

Main Street from Shelton Square, showing Iroquois Hotel, Buffalo, N.Y.

This view south from Shelton Square showcases the prominent White Building and Weed Company Hardware, founded in the early 1830s. It also illustrates the somewhat common problem of incorrect captions on postcards. The Ellicott Square Building, not the Iroquois Hotel, is seen on the left. The automobiles reveal this postcard to have been taken in the 1920s

Main Street on a Busy Day, Buffalo, N.Y.
Pedestrians crowd the storefronts in this view of Main Street at Shelton Square looking south. Postmarked July 13, 1909, this postcard provides a peek at several prominent Buffalo businesses, including Fleischmann's, Snyder's, and Neiderpruem and Sons.

then sold the building to the Tri-State Realty Company several months later and it was slated to be renovated for use as a retail store and office building. Several name changes followed, as evidenced by postcards bearing pictures of the building.

A postcard dated 1914 pictures the building with an inscription across the top cornice identifying it as the Iroquois. Another postcard dating from the 1920s shows the building emblazoned with the title "Bramson Building." Finally, a photograph from 1938 shows the building with the name "Gerrans Building" inscribed across the top. The building was demolished in 1940.

The Erie County Bank was built in 1893 at Shelton Square on the site of the First Presbyterian Church. This nine-story red granite building contained 140 offices. The floors throughout the corridors were marble, as were the wall linings and counter fronts. Office floors were constructed of polished Georgia pine and the woodwork throughout the building was mahogany. The first floor was occupied by the Erie County Savings Bank and the Fidelity Trust and Guaranty Co. This extraordinary building was demolished in 1968 to make way for the Main Place Mall.

Although Shelton Square of the early 1900s no longer exists, the location continues to be a center of prominence in the city. Main Place Mall, M&T Plaza, the Erie Community College campus and the NFTA Bus Terminal are nearby as are the courts, law offices and business offices. Crowds throng the area on weekdays at the lunch hour.

Shopping District, Main St., Buffalo, N.Y.
The east side of Main Street, looking south. J. N. Adam & Co. on the left is one of several businesses featured in this view. The Iroquois Hotel, at the corner of Main and Eagle streets, is the large building in the background.

Lobby, Hotel Statler, Buffalo
The original Hotel Statler at Washington and Swan streets had an elegant interior lobby, supporting its claim as a world-class hotel.

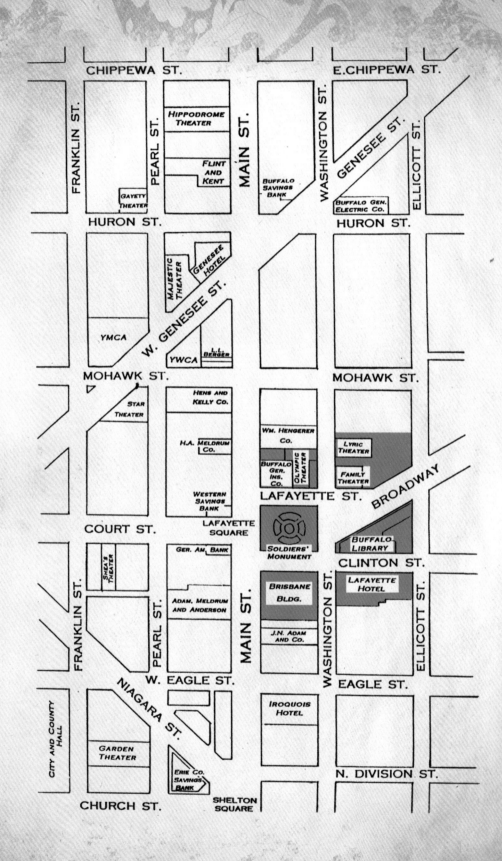

Chapter 5

LAFAYETTE SQUARE

Lafayette Square is a key point of convergence in Joseph Ellicott's radial street design. It was dedicated to Marquis Lafayette following his visit to Buffalo in 1825, and remains a focal point in the life of downtown Buffalo today.

The impressive statue that soars 85 feet over Lafayette Square is known as the Soldiers' and Sailors' Monument. It was dedicated "to the memory of the many people" who died while serving the United States in the armed forces. Grover Cleveland was present, as mayor of Buffalo, when the cornerstone was laid in 1882 and again, as governor of New York State, when the monument was dedicated on July 4, 1884. The impressive monument features four bronze statues around the base and a statue of the Goddess of Liberty on top; it was built at a cost of $50,000.

Lafayette Square, Buffalo, N.Y.

Lafayette Square, the point at which Clinton Street and Broadway converge with Main Street. Soldiers and Sailors Monument, erected to commemorate veterans, was dedicated on July 4, 1884, and is the centerpiece of Lafayette Square. The Brisbane Building, the Lafayette Hotel and a portion of the Erie County Library are all visible.

What's In a Name?

Accurate history rests in the details, and a study of Main Street is ample proof of this. Both the names and the addresses have changed quite radically from the early days.

Joseph Ellicott was commissioned by the Holland Land Company to survey the village of Buffalo and to lay out the radial street design. Many of the early street names were of Dutch or Native American origin, and thus quite difficult to pronounce. This led the Board of Trustees in July 1826 to change many names, as recorded in Larned's History of Buffalo:

Willink & Van Stophurst Avenue to Main Street

North & South Oneida Street to Ellicott Street

North & South Onondaga Street to Washington Street

North & South Cayuga Street to Pearl Street

Tuscarora Street to Franklin Street

Vollenhoven Avenue to Erie Street

Schimelpennick Avenue to Niagara Street

Busti Avenue to Genesee Street

Cazenovia Avenue to Court Street

(continued on page 43)

The classic Renaissance style Brisbane Building was completed in 1895. It was built on the site of the Arcade Building, which stood on the south side of Lafayette Square until it was devastated by fire on December 14, 1893. The location was highly sought after because of its proximity to hotels, major department stores and banks.

Although built by James Brisbane and James Mooney, Mr. Brisbane assumed full control of the building in 1906. Three major stores occupied the building by 1908. The well-known Buffalo clothier, the Kleinhans Co., occupied the portion of the first floor that faced Lafayette Square. The remainder of the first floor was occupied by Faxon, Williams and Faxon, grocers, and S. H. Knox's 5 & 10 cent store. These stores had entrances on both Main and Washington streets. The building's upper floors housed the offices of life insurance companies, major railroads and law firms.

Construction of the Lafayette Hotel was announced in early 1900, but it did not open its doors until June 1, 1904. It was built in the French Renaissance style and construction costs totaled approximately $1 million. The many public spaces throughout the seven-story building were designed in French styles, including Louis XIV, Louis XV, and First Empire, and many of the nearly 300 guest rooms had a bath or a shower. The hotel's location on the southeast corner of Washington and Clinton streets, opposite Lafayette Square, was excellent. Trolley cars to transport guests to Niagara Falls, Olcott Beach, Lancaster, Lockport, Hamburg and other suburban communities were just a two-minute stroll from the impressive front entrance.

Buffalo's earliest library was a six-story building on the corner of Main and Eagle. When it was remodeled in 1864, it also became the home of the Young Men's Association and soon also housed the Association's library. The building was again remodeled in 1886 as the Richmond Hotel. Only a few months later, it burned together with St. James Hall, which stood directly behind it on East Eagle Street. The Iroquois Hotel was built on this site in 1889, and the Buffalo and Erie County Library was erected on Lafayette Square. This massive structure served as the city's library and public meeting space until it was demolished in the early 1960s and replaced by the current Buffalo and Erie County Library building.

The German Insurance Company was established in 1867 and the five-story iron building at 447 Main Street that it occupied was completed in 1875. The company served generations of Buffalonians.

The Western Savings Bank, founded in 1851, was the second savings bank in Buffalo. Originally located on Seneca Street near Main, the bank moved several times in a fairly brief period before moving to a new building on the northwest corner of Main and Court streets.

The German American Bank opened in the basement of the Erie County Savings Bank building on the southwest corner of Main and Court streets on May 10, 1882. In 1883, the bank moved to 440 Main Street and later expanded its space at that address. A subsequent move returned the bank to its original building on the southwest corner of Main and Court streets and, in 1893, it took over the entire building. In fact, the bank's expansion went beyond its walls. After changing its name to Liberty Bank on April 15, 1918, in response to sentiments associated with the Great War (World War I), it began opening branch offices. By the early 1920s, Liberty Bank had no fewer than four branches in Buffalo. Yet another expansion in the mid-1920s resulted in the construction of the Liberty Bank Building, which still stands at 422 Main Street.

To add to the confusion, the street numbers on Main Street were changed in 1867 so that the street number multiplied by ten gives the distance in feet from the Buffalo River!

Perhaps the most interesting name change involves a church. When the Lafayette Presbyterian Church moved from Lafayette Square to its new location at the northeast corner of Bouck and Elmwood Avenue on May 10, 1896, the church trustees thought it appropriate to bring the street name along with the move. The City Council changed the name from Bouck to Lafayette Avenue.

Main Street & Lafayette Square, Buffalo, N.Y.
For comparison with the previous postcard, a later postcard of Lafayette Square shows the influence of the automobile. By 1925, the square has been converted to a traffic circle and much of its early charm has been covered by pavement.

Buffalo, N.Y., Lafayette Hotel

The Lafayette Hotel, which opened on June 1, 1904. Built in the French Renaissance style, the hotel had nearly three hundred rooms and was one of the largest and finest hotels in Buffalo.

Lafayette Square, Showing Soldiers & Sailors Monument, Buffalo, N.Y.

A close-up of the Soldiers and Sailors Monument in Lafayette Square. The Brisbane Building, built in 1895, is also clearly visible. Kleinhans, a well-known men's clothing store, was the building's primary business occupant for many years.

Buffalo Public Library, Buffalo, N. Y.

Buffalo Public Library, Buffalo, N.Y.
The grand structure which housed the Buffalo and Erie County Library was constructed in the early 1890s
on Lafayette Square. Postmarked December 7, 1910, this postcard shows the full magnitude of the building, which
was demolished in 1963 to make way for the modern structure which currently serves as the Central Library of the
Buffalo and Erie County Public Library system.

Lafayette Square, Public Library and Monument, Buffalo, N. Y.

Lafayette Square, Public Library and Monument, Buffalo, N.Y.
The public library at the junction of Broadway (on the left) and Clinton streets. These main thoroughfares
radiated out from Lafayette Square.

German Insurance Building, Lafayette Square, Buffalo, N.Y
  The north side of Lafayette Square. The German Insurance Building, built in 1875, the Olympic Theatre
(red building) and the Family Theatre (gray building) are all clearly visible.

North on Main St. from Court St., Buffalo, N.Y.
  The German Insurance Building and Wm. Hengerer's columned store, a retail icon for many years, are pictured
on the right side of Main Street. On the left side is the Western Savings Bank at 438 Main on the northwest corner of
Court Street. The domed Buffalo Savings Bank can be seen in the far background.

Court St., Shea's Theatre & McKinley Monument, Buffalo, N.Y.

This view is down Court Street from Lafayette Square to Niagara Square and the McKinley Monument. Note in the background the absence of City Hall, which was not built until the early 1930s. Shea's Court Theatre on the left was the first theater managed by Michael Shea. It opened in 1904.

Main and Court Street, Buffalo, N.Y. The Yellow Car for Niagara Falls

This picture was taken at Lafayette Square looking west on Court Street. The German American Bank, which changed its name to Liberty Bank in 1918, stood on the current site of the Liberty Building. The electric trolleys ran from Lafayette Square all the way to Niagara Falls!

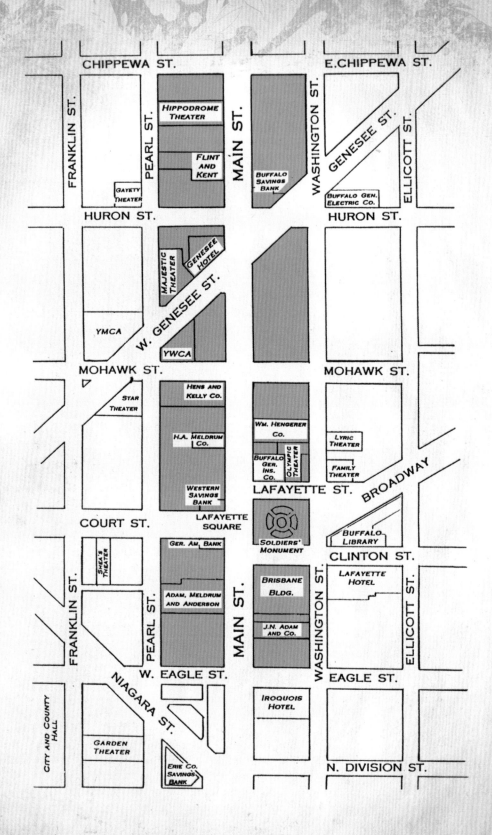

Chapter 6

THE SHOPPING DISTRICT

Main Street from Eagle Street on the south end to Chippewa Street on the north end — including Lafayette Square — was a bustling shopping and entertainment district in 1910.

Many large department stores and theatres lined both sides of Main, and postcards show crowds frequenting these venues. This was a time when a day of leisure meant a day downtown, when department stores played a prominent role in the lives of Buffalonians.

One of the features of a growing city is the rapid emergence — and disappearance — of small retail stores. Some grew and stayed in business for a considerable time. Growth meant absorbing neighboring stores, moving to more spacious sites, or constructing larger establishments. In Buffalo, the latter two options routinely involved a move northward on Main Street. The old premises frequently became the site of a new company or one in an earlier stage of expansion.

Bird's-eye View of the H. A. Meldrum Company's Department Stores 460-470 Main Street Buffalo, N.Y.
This prominent shopping area on the west side of Main Street was known as "the American block," and was
home to the H. A. Meldrum Company's department stores. Postmarked November 16, 1911

*Buffalo was a city of rapid
growth in the late 1800s. It was
a time when entrepreneurs, men
of vision, talent and financial
resources—men like Stephen Van
Rensselaer Watson—flourished on
what was then the frontier.*

*Watson was a prominent banker,
but he also founded the Buffalo
Street Railroad Company. In
1860, the first streetcar lines using
horse-drawn trolleys ran up Main
Street from the Buffalo River to
Genesee Street. Electric-powered
trolleys on rails followed later.*

*The early days of the company
were a major financial drain
on Watson, the principal
stockholder. From 1860 to 1867,
the company laid more new track
than it had means to pay for
and borrowed all the money it
could on bonds and promissory
notes. Only over time were all
the debts paid. It was Watson's
vision and determination that
allowed the company to expand
and eventually become a major
contributor to the city's growth in
the early 1900s.*

*The Hon. E. Carlton Sprague
gave elegant testimony to Watson
in the language of the day
following his death: "He never
reaped the rewards of his labors.
He never enjoyed even the sight of
the promised land, except through
the telescope of his imagination."*

*Watson's mansion on Delaware
Avenue was sold to The
Buffalo Club in 1870, and this
architectural treasure is preserved
today as an elegant part of the
club's facilities.*

The Flint and Kent department store is a perfect illustration of this process. In 1832, Benjamin Fitch opened a dry goods store at 188 Main Street near the Terrace. Business was so good that by 1835, Benjamin called his brother William to come from Connecticut to help him. New partners then began adding their names to the business. It became Fitch and Howard in 1844, and Howard, Whitcomb and Co. in 1855. After two additional interim name changes, it finally became Flint and Kent in 1865. By this time, these two men were the principal owners. Expansion brought a move in 1856 to a larger store at 207 Main Street, between Exchange and Seneca streets. Further growth led to yet another move to 261-263 Main Street, between Seneca and Swan streets, and finally in 1897, to a new four-story building built by the company at 554-562 Main Street, between Huron and Chippewa streets. A newspaper article in 1932 noted that the new store had forty-six departments, each of which was larger than the original store in 1832. Incorporated as Flint and Kent in 1909, the firm had ceased operations by 1966.

Another good example of this process is the William Hengerer Co., said to be the descendent of a store that started in 1836. It is at least clear that in April 1861, Hamlin and Madsen established a dry goods store at 256-258 Main Street, between Seneca and Swan streets. Shortly after the end of the Civil War, the proprietors were Falkner, Potts and Jackson, who were succeeded in 1886 by Barnes and Bancroft. This store then became Barnes and Hengerer, and in 1895, the William Hengerer Co. was incorporated.

A fine, six-story brick structure was built at 256-258 Main Street in 1889, and it housed the William Hengerer Co. until the store relocated in 1904 to 465 Main Street. When Hengerer's expanded and moved uptown, the site at 256-258 Main Street was completely remodeled. On May 4, 1904, the old building was occupied by the newly formed Sweeney Co. The motto of the new company was "A reliable quality of merchandise cheap for cash," and the company referred to itself as "the Store of the People." The interconnected nature of the merchandising community is clear from the fact that capital for the investment was provided by John F. Sweeney, who was president of the H. A. Meldrum Co.; Herbert A. Meldrum, secretary and treasurer of the same company; and William Hamlin, a local capitalist. The Hamlin estate owned the building in which the store was located.

Main Street, The Wm. Hengerer Co's Department Store, Buffalo, N.Y.

Main Street, The Wm. Hengerer Co's Department Store, Buffalo, N.Y.
The Wm. Hengerer Co.'s department store. Originally at 256-268 Main Street, it moved in 1904 to the site of the Tifft Hotel, which was demolished after it passed to the Tifft estate.

This building at 256-258 Main Street was converted to office use in 1965. The various changes in occupancy were accompanied by significant changes in the appearance of the building, especially its façade. In 1990, the building was restored as a landmark in the Joseph Ellicott Historic Preservation District.

The site at 465 Main Street to which Hengerer's moved in 1904, was originally the location of the Phoenix Hotel, built in 1816. This old-fashioned frame structure became famous as a meeting place in the early days of the city. It was replaced by the more substantial Tifft House in 1865. Although it was originally intended to be a boarding house, citizens petitioned George Tifft to make his new establishment into a hotel after the American Hotel burned on January 25, 1865. Tifft agreed, and the Tifft House became, for many years, the finest hotel in the city. The Tifft estate sold the property and the building was demolished in 1902.

Hengerer's opened at this location in 1904 and remained an important department store for most of the twentieth century. In recent memory, the company was sold and successively renamed Sibley's, Sibley's-Kaufmann's, Kaufmann's-Sibley's, and finally just Kaufmann's. Both of these chains were subsidiaries of the May Department Stores Co. of St. Louis.

The American Hotel opened in 1836 on the west side of Main Street between Court and Eagle streets. After just fourteen years, it burned down on May 10, 1850, but was quickly rebuilt. Abraham Lincoln visited this new iteration of the American en route to his first inauguration in 1861. But the new structure lasted only fifteen years before it, too, was destroyed by fire on January 25, 1865. A commercial building was then built on this site. It was called the American Block, after the hotels that had preceded it.

It was on the American Block that the retail enterprise of Adam, Meldrum and Anderson began operations in 1867. Although this first store at 396-400 Main Street was just twenty-two feet wide, it boasted eleven employees. Only $77 worth of merchandise was sold between eight o'clock in the morning and eight o'clock in the evening on the first day of operations, March 21, 1867. This was hardly an impressive amount, even for that time. The shop would nonetheless ultimately become a very successful department store.

Genesee Hotel, Buffalo, N.Y.
The Genesee Hotel on the northwest corner of Genesee and Main streets, facing Genesee Street. Built in 1882, this imposing structure was razed in 1922 to make way for the Genesee Building, now the site of the Hyatt Regency Hotel.

The firm started as a partnership of Robert B. Adam, Herbert A. Meldrum and Alexander Whiting. Whiting withdrew in 1872, and in 1876, William Anderson became a new partner. Although the name remained the same until modern times, by the turn of the century only the Adam Family was still involved in the business. The venture had just three active presidents during its first century of operation, and all were named Robert Borthwick Adam.

The first Robert Borthwick Adam, who served from 1833 through 1904, was born in Peebles, Scotland. He left school at age ten and became an apprentice to a notions and fabric exporter in Edinburgh, Scotland. He was later recruited by the Boston firm of Hogg, Brown, and Taylor, who brought him to the United States for employment. By age thirty-four, he had saved some money and was ready to establish his own store. He chose to launch the venture in Buffalo, and Hogg, Brown and Taylor matched his savings. He was successful, but he had no children, so he adopted a nephew and a niece. The nephew's name was Robert B. Scott, but he took the name Robert Borthwick Adam upon adoption. He lived from 1863 until 1940 and served as the second president of the company from 1904 through 1940. His son, of the same name, succeeded him as president; he lived from 1918 until 1993. All three Robert Borthwick Adams are buried in Buffalo's Forest Lawn Cemetery.

In 1879, after twelve years in business, the first Robert Borthwick Adam wrote to his younger brother and urged him to join him in Buffalo to establish another department store. J. N. Adam arrived in Buffalo in 1881 and opened his first store, J. N. Adam & Co. in the White Building at 292-298 Main Street, just south of Shelton Square. The company expanded rapidly. In 1891, it relocated to 387-389 Main Street, just south of Lafayette Square and across the street from Adam, Meldrum and Anderson. By 1908, the store had expanded to occupy three contiguous buildings, 383-393 Main Street, and had several warehouses and a stable, as well.

In addition to being a successful businessman, J. N. Adam became mayor of Buffalo. The store he founded had passed from family ownership by the time it closed in 1960. The building was then occupied by AM&A.

By the end of 1966, AM&A had six suburban stores and another location on the way in addition to its main downtown store. In 1994, the AM&A chain of ten stores was bought by BonTon stores. The downtown store at 389 Main Street was closed on March 18, 1995. The Buffalo News noted the next day that this closing was the latest and probably the most prominent entry in the list of downtown closings, which already included Hengerer's, Hens and Kelly, Kobacher's, Flint and Kent, Ulbrich's, L. L. Berger, and W. T. Grant. AM&A had been a downtown anchor for 128 years.

The H. A. Meldrum Co. was established in 1897. It was a large establishment at 460-470 Main Street, between Court and Mohawk streets, and across Main from the W. M. Hengerer Co. In 1922, it was bought out by the Edwards Co., which had started in 1832 in Johnstown, New York. Daniel, the founder's son, expanded the business to Troy, Syracuse and Rochester. The Troy venture ended when the company moved to Buffalo in 1922.

Majestic Theatre and Genesee Hotel, Buffalo, N.Y.

Majestic Theatre and Genesee Hotel, Buffalo, N.Y.
The Majestic Theatre and the Genesee Hotel, viewed from Pearl Street looking east. The Majestic and the hotel are west of Main Street, while the Buffalo Savings Bank in the background is across the way on the east side of Main.

In 1926, Edwards built a warehouse and furniture showroom on a site bordered by Pearl, Franklin, and Genesee streets. Business continued at both locations until Daniel Edwards died in 1929. The company moved all operations to the new building in the mid-1930s. On December 27, 1952, it was the first of the major local department stores in Buffalo to close.

Main Street, North of Huron Street, Buffalo, N.Y.

Main Street, North of Huron Street, Buffalo, N.Y.
Buffalonians flocking to Main Street to shop in the bustling downtown shopping district north of Huron Street. The Flint and Kent Department Store, at 554 Main Street, is on the left, and the soaring steeple of St. Louis Church is visible in the far background.

Hens and Kelly Co. was founded in 1892 at 478-488 Main Street, on the southwest corner of Main and Mohawk, known as the "Miller Block." On June 29, 1922, the Times stated:

"It was 32 years ago that M. J. Hens and P. J. Kelly started the Hens and Kelly store. The first store was in a building, on the present site, 60 x 18. So rapidly did the business grow that in only five weeks, Hens and Kelly took over another building, adjoining, the same size as their original. And the store has been growing ever since. Nineteen years ago (i.e.1903) Hens & Kelly bought through the entire block to Pearl Street, giving the store the corner frontage in Main, Mohawk, and Pearl streets, with the wonderful advantage of having display windows on all three busy streets."

Kleinhans, another important clothier in Buffalo, was founded by Edward L. Kleinhans and his brother. The first store opened for business on May 10, 1893, at 259 Main Street between Seneca and Swan. Two years later, Kleinhans moved to the Brisbane Building on Lafayette Square, where it remained until it closed on December 3, 1992, nearly a century later. The building has since been remodeled and is currently an office building. However, Edward

Gayety Theatre, Buffalo, N.Y.

Buffalo in its heyday boasted many theaters, and may in fact be the birthplace of the purpose-built motion picture theater. The Gayety Theatre was constructed in 1915 at the northwest corner of Huron and Pearl streets, one block off Main Street in the current Theater District.

Entrance, Shea's Hippodrome, Buffalo, N.Y.

Buffalo Optical, at 574 Main Street, and Shea's Hippodrome Theatre, a favorite destination for Buffalo theatergoers. Both are on the west side of Main Street.

Kleinhans' legacy lives on in Buffalo. Kleinhans served as president of the stores that bore his name until his death in 1934, when the bulk of his estate was dedicated to the construction of Kleinhans Music Hall.

L. L. Berger opened a fine clothing store for women at 500 Main Street in 1905. L. L. Berger, as the store was known, expanded to 514 Main Street in 1926, completed an addition there in 1942, and after World War II constructed a new eight-story building at that address. Berger owned five stores by the time L. L. Berger went out of business in February 1991.

Buffalo Savings Bank, Buffalo, N.Y.
The Buffalo Savings Bank, with its iconic gold leaf dome, was completed in 1900 at the junction of Main,
Genesee and Huron streets.

Seymour Knox and his cousin, Frank Woolworth, were the founders of a special kind of store. After Woolworth opened his first 5 & 10 cent store in Watertown, New York, its success prompted the cousins to open a similar store in Lancaster, Pennsylvania. Shortly thereafter, in 1888, Knox came to Buffalo to open his own store. The first store in the Knox chain was in the Wonderland Building, also called the Arcade, at Main and Lafayette Square. Although there was a fire at the Arcade on December 14, 1893, Knox reopened at 519 Main Street, between Mohawk and Huron streets, within just a matter of days and managed to do a brisk Christmas business. Knox moved the store into the Brisbane Building in 1895, after it was built on the site of the old Arcade.

The success of this type of store led Knox and Woolworth to form a syndicate in 1896 to run their growing empires, headquartered in the Prudential Building in Buffalo. By 1912, Knox had ninety-eight stores in the United States and thirteen stores in Canada. The Knox and Woolworth chains merged that year, marking the start of the F. W. Woolworth Co. Woolworth built the Woolworth Building in New York City with his personal funds. At the time, it was the tallest building in the world. This accomplishment is a fair indication of the wealth he had generated. When construction was completed, the syndicate's head offices moved there.

Knox maintained his interests in Buffalo and became quite prominent in the banking community. He was instrumental in the merger of Columbia National Bank and Marine National Bank, which eventually became the Marine Trust Co.

The Woolworth stores in the U.S. were closed in two stages. In 1994, approximately 970 stores in the United States and Canada closed. A 1997 Buffalo News article noted: "When the F. W. Woolworth store at 395 Main Street closes its doors for good later this year, a 102-year tradition of variety store retailing in downtown Buffalo will come to an end."

Try to imagine walking up the west side of Main Street in 1910, when it was a thriving shopping district lined with these stately department stores. Start at Eagle, stroll on to Court (at Lafayette Square), then pass Mohawk and Genesee (diagonal) streets, continue on to Huron and finally end up at Chippewa Street. Note that as these streets cross Main Street, their names change from west to east; only Virginia Street remains the same on both sides of Main Street.

Central High School, Buffalo, N.Y.
Central High School was the city's first building devoted exclusively to education for grades nine through twelve. It was located downtown, bordering Niagara Square at Delaware Court, two blocks west of the shopping district.

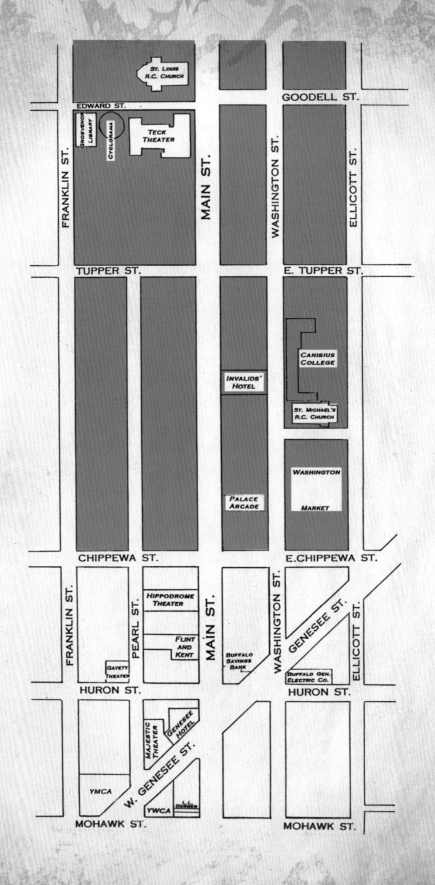

Chapter 7

Upper Main Street

Main Street becomes less dense between Chippewa and Edward (on the west side) and Goodell (on the east side). The Chippewa Market, also called Washington Market, was a large outdoor venue for farmers and food sellers with literally hundreds of stalls. It covered the entire city block bordered by Washington, Chippewa, and Ellicott Streets and by St. Michael's Church on the north side. Moving northward, the area became more industrial, and several breweries were situated just north of Goodell on the east side of Main Street.

There were also a number of prominent buildings in this section of Main Street. Canisius High School/College and St. Michael's Church, both founded by the Jesuits, were just one block east of Main on Washington Street. Canisius began in 1870 as a school for young men. The College moved to its present location on Main Street at Jefferson in 1910. The high school remained on Washington until it moved to Delaware Avenue in 1944.

Main Street, showing Dr. Pierce's Dispensary, Buffalo, N.Y.
Invalids' Hotel and Surgical Institute, at 665 Main Street, was one of the first private hospitals in the country. It was built by Dr. Ray V. Pierce, one of the most successful and high-profile medical doctors of the time. The building was demolished in 1941.

The fascinating story behind the Palace Hotel for invalids and tourists, which faced Prospect Park, revolves around the enterprising Dr. Ray Vaughn Pierce. Born in the Herkimer County town of Stark, New York, on August 6, 1840, Dr. Pierce graduated from the Eclectic Medical College of Cincinnati in 1862. He practiced medicine in Pennsylvania for four years before moving to Buffalo in 1867. Dr. Pierce soon began preparing and selling proprietary medicines, such as "Dr. Pierce's Favorite Prescription." These products brought him both success and a degree of renown.

Dr. Pierce opened the Palace Hotel on Porter Avenue for invalids and tourists in 1870. A large, impressive Victorian building, it lays claim to the first elevator in the city. After it was destroyed by fire in 1881, he replaced it with the Invalids' Hotel and Surgical Institute at 665 Main Street, between Chippewa and Tupper streets. The facility remained there until 1941.

Chippewa Market, Buffalo, N.Y.
The Chippewa Market, also known as the Washington Street Market, was a popular outlet for area farmers. The block was bordered by Washington, Chippewa and Ellicott streets, and by St. Michael's Church to the north.

Dr. Pierce was one of the most notable patent-medicine doctors of the time. Between 1867 and 1880, he shipped nearly a million bottles of his preparations out of Buffalo annually and took in approximately half a million dollars a year! His products bore catchy names, like Dr. Pierce's Smart Weed and Dr. Pierce's Pleasant Pellets. The good doctor also wrote and sold a volume called *The People's Common Sense Medical Advisor in Plain English*, which ran to as many as one hundred editions during the sixty years it remained in print. Extensive advertising resulted in a large mail-order business. The medicines were prepared in a laboratory at 664 Washington Street under the direction of Dr. Pierce's son, who was also a physician.

Genesee, Chippewa and Washington Streets, Buffalo, N.Y.
The streets close to Main were busy commercial areas, as well. This scene looks north on Washington Street,
with St. Michael's Church in the background. Buffalo Savings Bank at the intersection of Main, Genesee and
Huron streets can be seen in the upper left corner.

In addition to working as a physician, purveyor of medicines, and author, Dr. Pierce also served as a state senator and, later, as a member of the U.S. House of Representatives.

The Music Hall, or Teck Theatre, offers interesting insights into the German community at this time. The North American Saengerbund, a German choral society, started circa 1829, and the first Saengerfest was held in Cincinnati in 1840. There was much rivalry over the location of the biennial Saengerfest, principally among Chicago, St. Louis, and Cincinnati. In 1860, however, it was held in Buffalo in the old New York Central Depot on Exchange Street. When it was decided in 1881 to have the twenty-third Fest in Buffalo in 1883, the German Young Men's Association knew that a large hall would be needed. The leaders of the Association raised $235,000 and bought the homestead of Ebenezer Walden at Main and Edward, where the first theater was built. The Twenty-Third Fest in July 1883 boasted three thousand singers and an orchestra of one hundred musicians under the direction of Leopold Damrosch.

The music hall was lost in a fire that also destroyed St. Louis Church on March 25, 1885. A new music hall was built on the site and was rededicated on February 7, 1888.

The building carried a heavy debt when it was sold to J. F. Schoellkopf for $6,000 in July, 1899. After being remodeled, it reopened as the Teck Theatre on September 4, 1900. The building was owned by the Schoellkopf estate, and it is said that the theater's new name was derived from the fact that the late Jacob F. Schoellkopf was born in Kirchheim-on-Teck in Germany. The Old Teck was razed in 1942.

The first Catholic church in Buffalo was not St. Joseph's Cathedral as is commonly thought. That distinction actually belongs to St. Louis Church. On January 5, 1829, Louis Etienne Le Couteulx gave Bishop DuBois of New York property at the corner of Main and Edward streets for a church, school, rectory and cemetery. A simple log structure dedicated to the "Lamb of God" was built there in 1831. In 1843, a large brick church was built around the old building, but burned down on March 25, 1885. Construction began the following year on the imposing structure that still stands at that site today. The first services were held in the new church in August 1889.

Early Morning Chippewa Market, Buffalo, N.Y.
Postmarked 1908, this postcard provides a look at the common dress of the day as shoppers and vendors conduct business along the Ellicott Street façade of the busy Chippewa Market.

St. Louis was also the scene of some friction between the pastor and church trustees, who wanted more control over the church's funds. Bishop Hughes of New York ended up forbidding services at the church for some time. Eventually, the parties reconciled their differences.

In 1857, visionary Seth Grosvenor bequeathed $40,000 to Buffalo, designating $10,000 of it for the purchase of a lot and building, and the remainder for the endowment of a library. The library was to be open to the public and for reference use only, which is how the Grosvenor Library became part of the public library system. The money was paid to the city in 1865 with the understanding that the city would pay for the library's yearly operating expenses.

The library actually opened in 1870 in rooms in the Buffalo Savings Bank Building. By 1891, the invested money had increased sufficiently to allow for the construction of a new building at Franklin and Edward streets. By 1908, the library housed 75,000 volumes and 7,000 pamphlets for reference.

Canisius College, Buffalo, N.Y.
    Canisius College, founded by the Jesuits in 1870, was originally located on Washington Street north of
St. Michael's Church and directly across the street from the back of Dr. Pierce's Invalids' Hotel.

Teck Theatre, Buffalo, N.Y.
    The Teck Theatre at 760 Main Street, on the site of the old Buffalo Music Hall. St. Louis Church can be seen in
the background.

There is no postcard here that shows the Market Arcade (called the Palace Arcade in the 1915 City Atlas), but the building was prominent in life along Main Street at this time. This building was restored in the 1990s and is beautifully described on a plaque on the building at 617 Main Street:

"From the massive buffalo heads which punctuate each entry archway of its twin facades on Main and Washington streets, to the soaring classical elegance of the triple-tiered atrium inside, the Market Arcade must have seemed a most extraordinary place from the moment it opened in 1892. Philanthropist/builder George B. Matthews anticipated the modern indoor shopping mall, wanting a commercial building that functioned as an 'indoor street' of sorts, offering a variety of small shops and offices protected from inclement weather. He also wanted to connect Main Street and its trolley traffic to the Chippewa Market, the city's major market of the time (hence the building's name).

St. Louis Church, Main & Edward Sts., Buffalo, N.Y.

"Using London's Burlington Arcade as its design inspiration, the local architectural firm of Green and Wicks created this Beaux-Arts masterpiece. Aside from its unusual design and fine ornamentation inside and out, it was also one of the city's first completely fireproof buildings due to its construction of steel, glass, brick, and concrete. Also noteworthy is its maximization of natural light, evidenced by huge frosted skylights and glass blocks on the upper tier walkways that allow light through to the first floor. The building's shops featured large plate glass windows in which merchandise could be attractively displayed, a relatively new retailing concept at the time. In its intimate scale and elaborate neoclassical details, the Market Arcade was a treasured Main Street landmark for generations of Buffalonians, and can now be enjoyed again due to a major restoration."

St. Louis Church, Main & Edward Sts., Buffalo, N.Y.
St. Louis Church, one of the largest and oldest churches in the Buffalo Catholic Diocese.

THE GROSVENOR LIBRARY, BUFFALO, N. Y.

The Grosvenor Library, Buffalo, N.Y.
The Grosvenor Library at the corner of Franklin and Edward streets, directly behind the Teck Theatre.

The Market Arcade has been owned by the City of Buffalo since being closed in the 1970s. In 1978, it was designated a local landmark. In the early 1990s, approximately $9 million in public funding was invested in restoring the Market Arcade and the two buildings and three facades (all pre-1920) adjacent to it, to create the Market Arcade complex. Designated by New York State as an urban cultural park, the complex is home to the "Theater District Visitor Center" and a variety of office and specialty tenants.

From the Market Arcade to Tupper Street is an area of Main Street that is now called the Theater District. In 1910, this section was at the fringe of the business district, and it was not until the 1920s that prominent buildings like Shea's Buffalo Theater were erected.

So ends our illustrated walk up Main Street, from the Buffalo River to Edward Street. How fitting that postcards, made popular during Buffalo's heyday, pave the way through the city's illustrious past. Perhaps they also provide valuable clues for directions in which Buffalo's beautiful downtown could and should develop a century hence, rising from the ashes to emerge once again as a vital, vibrant hub for the entire region.

Postcard Index

Sources

Barry, John F., and Robert W. Elmes, eds. *Buffalo's Textbook, 1928, Board of Education.* Buffalo, NY: Robert W. Elmes, 1924.

Buffalo 1908: A History of the City of Buffalo, Illustrated. Buffalo, NY: Buffalo Evening News, 1908.

Carline, Richard. *Pictures in the Post: The Story of the Picture Postcard and its Place in the History of Popular Art.* Philadelphia: Deltiologists of America, 1972.

Larned, J. N. *A History of Buffalo,* Vol. 1, New York City: Progress of the Empire State Company, 1911.

Paul's Dictionary of Buffalo, Niagara Falls, Tonawanda and Vicinity. Buffalo, NY: Peter Paul Book Company, 420 Main Street, 1896.

Rodder, Joseph H. *"Way of Public Transport from Horse Cars to Metro Rail."* Western New York Heritage Magazine, 8, 2: 52.

Rossi, Dale. *"Main Street: What Number is it?"* Western New York Heritage Magazine, 3, 2: 7.

Scrapbook Collection. Grosvenor Room, Buffalo & Erie County Public Library.